RETIREMENT INVESTING

101

A STEP BY STEP PROCESS FOR BUILDING AND MANAGING A RETIREMENT PORTFOLIO

RETIREMENT INVESTING
101

A STEP BY STEP PROCESS FOR BUILDING
AND MANAGING A RETIREMENT PORTFOLIO

By

Phillip Washington, Jr.

PW Media
Cedar Hill, Texas

RETIREMENT INVESTMENT 101
Published by:
PW Media
Cedar Hill, Texas
www.phillipwashingtonjr.com

Phillip Washington, Publisher
Warren Landrum, Editor
Yvonne Rose, QualityPress.info, Book Packager

DISCLAIMER
The information presented is for educational purposes and is not to be considered personal investment advice. The information is not to be considered a solicitation for the purchase of specific securities, investments or investment strategies. Investing involves risk and no investment is guaranteed unless so stated. Individuals viewing this presentation should speak with a qualified investment professional or tax adviser before acting on any information contained in this presentation.

Acknowledgements

Running a business is tough. I couldn't imagine doing it without the support of my partner in life, Kelley.

I've been able to build multiple businesses and help so many families feel confident about their financial future only because Kelley held down the home and gave me the air cover to work the hours necessary to be successful.

She also allowed me to make the investments necessary for our future that, at the time, I know wasn't easy and sometimes scary.

I also want to thank my parents, Phillip and Cheryl Washington, who instilled my character which I believe is the driving force behind the man I am today.

Thank you to Warren Landrum who mentored me through the process of writing this book and was my Editor.

Thank you as well to Ms. Yvonne Rose and her team at Quality Press for helping me package this book and getting it ready for publishing.

And last, but not least, I want to acknowledge my two boys, Tate and Kellen. Seeing your smiling faces brings me so much joy after long hard days of getting my face bashed in. I get up every day working hard to be a man you look up to and will forever be proud of.

Table of Contents

Introduction

Ray Dalio, the founder and Chief Investment Officer of the largest hedge fund in the world and who gives investment advice to the wealthiest people on the planet (like Bill Gates) said, "I'm a dumb shit who doesn't know much relative to what I need to know."

This statement embodies what's required to make money in financial markets... humility and lots of emotional intelligence.

I've been helping investors make investment decisions for over a decade now.

Along the way, I was blessed to have had some mentors who managed money for very wealthy families and had become wealthy themselves by following a well thought out investment plan.

I took what they said to heart and added to their wisdom by reading over 100 investment, business, and money books.

Their advice, plus what I've learned on my own, has helped me make some money for myself and clients I've given advice to over the years.

This short book is my best effort to share what I've learned over the years and share it in an easy-to-read format.

Since most of us didn't learn much about investing growing up, (I know I didn't) I start this book by wiping the slate of your mind clean by exposing 10 big investing myths that cause investors to make bad decisions.

After that, I show you how to build an investment portfolio for retirement, step by step.

Finally, you will learn why many investors underperform their own well-designed investment portfolios over the long term and what you can do to avoid that fate.

Now, instead of wasting any more time on this introduction, let's dive into how to make some money investing in stocks.

✣

PART 1

10 Big Investing Myths That Cause Investors to Make Bad Decisions

Investing Myth #1

⚜

I need a lot of money to start investing

I'm not going to give you an analogy of the benefits of just starting small and building up over time. You already know that.

If you really wanted to invest, all it would take is one or two phone calls to a bank, mutual fund company, financial advisor, or online investment broker to ask if you can start an investment account with whatever you can currently invest right now.

My guess is they would say, "Sure, let's get you set up." This is less of a myth and more of just an excuse to not start.

Here's one of my favorite Bible verses that I apply to money:

"If you are faithful in little things, you will be faithful in large ones. But if you are dishonest in little things, you won't be honest with greater responsibilities (Luke 16:10)."

Translation: If you can't put something away with the money you make now, making more money won't solve your problem.

Investing Myth #2

✠

I already have
a financial advisor

Most people I've talked to about investing that have a "financial advisor" are working with a sales representative, not an actual financial advisor. I'm not saying sales representatives are bad people. I was one for the first half of my career, before I fully understood the difference myself. I just want to educate investors on the difference because most people don't know there's a difference.

So, what is the difference?

Sales Representative

A sales representative is someone who gets paid to sell products.

Some products and companies pay them more. Some products and companies pay them less.

They are a representative of an investment broker.

Many sales representatives are restricted to selling only the products their investment broker allows them to sell.

There's no incentive to recommend some of the lower cost products (like low cost index funds and exchange traded funds) because they receive no money for recommending products that don't pay commission.

They are paid most of their money upfront for the products they sell and may get some trailing fees as long as you keep the product.

Financial Advisor

Financial advisors charge a fee for investment advice.

The fee charged is typically based on the account size, not which product he or she recommends.

The financial advisor works for you, not the investment broker.

The financial advisor recommends the investment options they believe will best help you reach your goals without worrying about broker limitations and big commission temptations.

Which would you prefer?

Here are some of the reasons I've heard from investors who say they prefer financial advisors over sales representatives:

- Financial products are complex. I don't have time to read through stacks of disclosures to know all the fees and commissions I'm being charged. I'm more comfortable paying someone to do that for me.
- I want objective advice, not advice that can be influenced by which company or product pays my "advisor" the most.
- What I pay my financial advisor is upfront and transparent. No hidden fees or costs.

Some financial professionals are financial advisors and sales representatives at the same time, meaning, they can sell investment products and can get paid a fee (I know, I know... just when it was starting to get a little less confusing.)

This is the main reason most people don't know the difference.

Their "financial advisor's" card will say financial advisor because they technically can charge a fee for advice. However, when I look at the portfolio they recommended to the investor I'm talking to, it's mostly, if not all, commission-based products that were sold.

When I break it down and explain it to people, many of them say they would prefer to work with a financial advisor over a sales representative.

Some, out of loyalty and not wanting to rock the boat, keep their sales representative.

That's okay too. I just want investors to understand the difference and make their own well-informed decision.

Investing Myth #3

✠

Stocks are too risky

Vanguard shares a study it did on its website showing the average annual growth of different portfolio mixes of stocks, bonds and cash from 1926 to 2016.

https://personal.vanguard.com/us/insights/saving-investing/model-portfolio-allocations

During that period, stocks grew at about 10.2% per year, meaning your money would have doubled roughly every 7 years on average.

During that same period, long-term U.S. government bonds grew at about 5.4% a year, with your money doubling every 13.33 years on average and U.S. cash grew at about 3.6% a year, with the money doubling every 20 years.

If the goal of investing is to one day generate a comfortable income from your investments so you work if you want to, not because you have to... (and if that's not your goal, let's grab coffee and talk about why that should be the goal,) then the safest long-term place for your money is stocks.

Not bonds or cash.

Stocks have been the best asset class for increasing your ability to buy more stuff later because it has historically allowed you to have more money in the future and therefore more of a cushion in your later years.

Let me put it another way.

Assume you have $100,000 today and you want to invest it for 30 years from now.

No one knows what returns will actually be over the next 30 years, but let's use history (which is all we have) as our guide.

If you invest your money 100% in stocks, in 30 years you should have roughly $1,842,671 assuming stocks earn their historic 10% annual growth average.

If you invest your money 100% in bonds, in 30 years you should have roughly $484,415 assuming bonds earn their historic 5.4% annual growth rate.

That's one-third less money by going the "safer" route instead of the more "risky" route.

(I'm intentionally not including what investing only in cash might grow to because those numbers are not even worth showing you.)

Now let me ask you a question.

Which account makes you feel more secure in your later years, the stock account or the bond account (more money or less money)?

Before I get someone emailing me saying, "But Phillip what if stocks don't earn 10% and what if bonds don't earn 5.4% over the next 30 years?"

Look, they probably won't earn exactly that. What I'm betting on is the relationship will stay the same over long term.

Stocks will very likely (because they have so far over the long term) earn more than bonds over a long period of time.

How am I so sure?

The same reason (in my best guess) that business owners, as a group, will likely continue to earn more money than employees, as a group.

The employee trades uncertainty for a guaranteed smaller paycheck.

The business owner embraces the uncertainty and provides a stable paycheck to his or her employees in exchange for a bigger, inconsistent paycheck.

It's all supply and demand.

In a capitalistic system like ours, if you provide a service that's in high demand and low supply, you get paid a lot for that service.

As long as most people hate the uncertainty of stocks in the short term, and you are willing to be an owner of stocks for the long term, you should continue to outperform the bond and cash owners over the long term.

It's really that simple of a concept, just not very easy emotionally to do.

P.S. I know there is a 60-year-old reading this and saying, "But Phillip, I don't have 30 years as my investment time horizon."

I will address this MYTH in a later section, Investing Myth #7.

⚜

Real estate is a better investment than stocks

This one is going to touch a few nerves here in Texas because everyone thinks they are a real estate mogul in the making.

Here is what I've heard many times over the years:

"Real estate is safer than stocks because they aren't making any more of it."

Or

"I only invest in real estate. It's safe. I can touch it."

(My face afterwards...☺. WTF...the F is for freak, pastor).

Sounds clever, but simply not true.

Instead of going the complex math route where I compare the long-term return of real estate versus stocks (which depends on how much leverage you are using to buy the property), I will put this myth to bed with a simpler approach.

First, who buys real estate?

Businesses and people.

The businesses need a place to sell their goods and services and people need places to live.

In general, the more prosperous the businesses and the employees of the businesses are, the higher the real estate prices move in that country, all other things being equal.

(Side note #1: Some people forget that stocks are shares of ownership in a business. So, when I am referring to businesses, I'm talking about stocks.)

If the "risky" or "inferior" businesses (stocks), go under, then so does the real estate market.

Stocks and real estate have historically moved up and down together over the long term.

When there's a recession, the price of stocks and real estate both go down.

When the economy is doing well, the price of stocks and real estate go up.

Let's look at it a different way.

Money has always gone and will likely always go to where it's treated the best in a capitalistic system ("Treated the best" translates: grows the most for a given level of risk.)

If real estate was the superior undisputed asset class, then all the money would have gone into real estate a long time ago.

If that happened, the price of real estate would have been bid up to a level where it was no longer attractive and could no longer be a "better" investment.

Then why do some people swear stocks are riskier?

Mostly ignorance.

Also, it's likely the fact that the property that they, own (or owned) doesn't have the price quoted to them every second of every day for 5 days a week like the price of publicly traded stocks.

Real estate investment trusts, commonly referred to as REITs, give you an idea of how your property would move if it was publicly traded.

(Side note #2: REITs are publicly traded companies that buy and sell real estate properties for their shareholders -basically, a publicly traded real estate investment partnership you participate in with other investors around the world.)

Look, there are billionaires who made their fortune investing in real estate and there are billionaires who made their fortune investing in businesses (stocks).

Both are excellent asset classes to own and even better to own together.

Diversification is one of the few time-tested ways to keep your money safe over the long term.

A wealthy mentor once shared with me his philosophy around investing, which he took from an ancient Jewish manuscript written back as early as 200 BC.

Here's what it says:

"Let every man divide his money into three parts, and invest a third in land, a third in business, a third let him keep in reserve."

My 2018 translation of that is, put a third of your money in real estate, a third in businesses (stocks), and a third in bonds and cash.

✠

To become a millionaire investor, I have to find the next "big thing"

One of my hobbies is studying the history of money, investing, business, and economics.

(I know...Nerd! When my wife is having trouble going to sleep, she tells me to turn on one of the economic podcasts I listen to weekly and she is out in 3 minutes flat.)

I like to look for principles that have always worked - principles you can apply to new investments and old investments.

As a wise man (King Solomon) once said, "There's nothing new under the sun."

Where am I going with this?

There have been wealthy investors for thousands of years. The majority of the investors didn't get wealthy by finding the next hot new industry.

They became wealthy by wisely putting their money to work to get the most return they could without risking a complete loss of all of their money (although quite a few had to lose a few fortunes along the way before they mastered that skill).

Let me explain what I mean, by using a banker as an example. (I'm using bankers because they have a long history of investing money. Banks came before public stocks, bonds, mutual funds, and hedge funds.)

You put your money with a bank because the banks tell you, they will keep your money safe and pay you a little interest today. They then turn around and use your money to lend it to people who need money to expand their businesses, buy real estate, go to college, pay for furniture, trips, etc.

Bankers have to be careful with how they invest your deposits because if they make bad loans with the money you entrusted them to keep safe, they are going out of business and a lot of bank customers will lose money (those with money above the FDIC limits).

How do they make sure they make money over time without losing your money?

The first thing they do is commit to not just making only a few big loans to a small amount of borrowers. The intelligent banker wants to make lots of loans across many different lines of business (business loans, real estate loans, credit cards, etc.).

That way if a few default, they won't lose all of the money they put to work.

The next thing the intelligent banker does is study the attributes of the borrower who pays on time and is a good credit risk in each line of business.

This takes lots of research, but with that info, they are able to build a screening process for the types of borrowers they want to do business with.

If someone is a higher risk, and the banker still wants to give them money, they can charge higher interest.

If someone is a very low risk, and the banker knows they have to compete to get their business from other bankers who want to put their money safely to work with that borrower, they have to charge lower interest.

One other thing that goes into the process is the banker looks at all the expenses that need to be paid to run the bank (i.e. interest paid to depositors, employee salaries, rent, marketing, etc.) and makes sure their loan portfolio makes enough money to pay all the bank's expenses, plus some for profit.

If they try to only lend to the safe credit risks, they likely won't earn enough to pay all their expenses and make a profit.

If they lend too much to risky borrowers, they risk having too many loans that default and take the bank down.

To make good long-term investments the banker, and his/her team, have to do their homework.

This is exactly how you should approach your long-term investing plan.

Here are a few examples of what my clients pay me to review and analyze before making an investment portfolio recommendation:

- Client's age
- Client's life expectancy
- Cash flow needs
- Current assets
- Current liabilities
- How much are they (the client) able to invest monthly/annually?
- What are the historical returns of different asset classes (stocks, bonds, cash, real estate, etc.)?
- How tight or loose money is in the global economy?
- What's going up and what's going down?
- Is the economy healthy?

- Is the political environment favorable for stocks, bonds, real estate, etc.?

- Are investors fearful, optimistic or euphoric?

- And much more...

(Side note: I spend a lot of money a year on a sophisticated software that helps me calculate the best probable outcome for a specific set of inputs. Many other financial advisors do the same thing for their clients before making investment recommendations (Real financial advisors, not sales representatives...see **Investing Myth #2: "I already have a financial advisor"***)***.*

Here's my point.

Making investment portfolio decisions without you yourself doing lots of homework and analysis or hiring someone to do it for you (and explain it to you) is a good way to stay out of the millionaire investors club (or get kicked out if you're already there).

"Only when the tide goes out do you discover who's been swimming naked."

- Warren Buffett

Investing Myth #6

⚜

My investments are fine.
I made money last year

Fellas, have you ever been on a couples' group date and thought the date was going real well until...you're driving away, and you look over at her with a smile?

You expect a smile back, but instead she hits you with that look (you know what look I'm talking about.)

You turn back to face the road thinking, "Dang, what happened!" (You start running through the night in your head.)

"We went to a nice restaurant, ordered appetizers, got separate entrees (no shared plates), desserts and drinks. Everyone was laughing, having a good time, and then..."

You remember that alcohol hitting your bloodstream and you made that one bad joke, that your lady kinda laughed at, but not really.

That's when you realize…" Yeah…. I F'ed up ☺."

What does this have to do with investing?

This is sort of what happens to investors over and over again.

Many investors think their investments are okay, when they really are in big trouble and don't realize it yet.

When you have an economy that's doing well, it's really not that difficult to make money in investing.

Everyone thinks their portfolio is "okay" because it's making money.

The problem is when there's a good economy you can probably throw a dart at a wall with random investment options on it and make money.

The goal in investing is to not just make money. **It's to make money and keep it.**

The investors who put the majority of their money in Enron stock in the early 2000s thought they were good, until the company went out of business.

The investors who put the majority of their money in newly created dot com companies in the late 1990s, thought they were good until the market came crashing down on them and wiped many of them completely out.

The investors who became real estate flipping experts after a weekend seminar and started buying real estate with no money down and borrowing to the max, thought they were good until money dried up, the real estate market tanked and took their credit scores with it.

Last one... (but I could go on for pages).

The U.S. stock market didn't perform well relative to its historic average from 2000 to 2009. Meanwhile emerging markets did quite well according to the MSCI emerging markets index over the same period.

I repeat. Successful investing is not just about making money.

It's about making it and keeping it.

The way you do that is by doing your homework and spreading your money out. No big bets. No shortcuts!

"In investing, what is comfortable is rarely profitable."

- Robert Arnott

Investing Myth #7

⚜

I have to figure out how to not lose money in a down market

Many investors worry too much about timing bear markets (periods of time when the market goes down 20% or more).

A bear market is a non-issue for a well-diversified investor building long-term wealth. The 30-year average return of the S&P 500 was roughly about 10% a year, meaning you would have roughly doubled your money every 7.2 years.

What bad things happened to the stock market during those 30 years?

- Black Monday 1987 when the stock market dropped about 20% in one day
- The bear market that happened at the end of 1990 (a roughly 20% drop)

- The technology bust from 2000 to 2002 (a roughly 49% drop)
- The financial crisis of 2007 to 2008 (a roughly 57% drop)

Let's imagine you invested $100,000 at the beginning of that 30-year period of time and your portfolio earned the same roughly 10% average annual return.

Today you would have about $1,744,940.

Your money grew to that amount despite the temporary setbacks in the stock market I referenced above.

The way you do your best to minimize risking your money to permanent loss is to spread your money out **(See Investing Myth #2)**.

Now I know there is someone thinking, "Well Phillip, what do I do if I need money during a bear market? I know it's not a good idea to pull money out of a portfolio that's going down."

Simple solution. Keep a reserve fund of cash and bonds.

The amount depends on your stage of life and your cash flow.

If you are still working you don't need as much in your reserve fund.

If you are retired and living on your money, think about having 5 years of your income in cash and bonds.

This will very likely provide you enough cash to draw on in really tough times (The average bear market lasts about 18 months based on my research.)

One last point for the folks who watched the Big Short, the movie about a few investors who timed the 2007 to 2008 bear market.

Yes, there are ways to basically "buy insurance" to protect your money from a down market (put options, stop losses, shorting, or using other complex derivatives).

The problem is "buying insurance" can cost you a lot of money if you are really off on your timing.

This can cause you to miss out on some of the returns that the market provides in bull markets (which happen more often than bear markets).

There are very rich investors who don't mind under-performing the market for VERY long periods of time to get the big payout whenever the market finally goes into a bear market.

Then there are investors like Warren Buffett, who don't mind bear markets because they have throughout history been temporary and have presented buying opportunities.

The point is there is no perfect investing strategy. You are going to experience pain either way.

The pain is why long-term, disciplined investors, who use a flawed approach that works over time, get rich.

They make their money from the investor looking for the "perfect system," straddling the fence of different strategies, and tapping out too early before pay day comes.

So, don't fear bear markets. See them for what they are.

The reason you will one day be wealthy if you follow a well-thought-out and well-diversified investment program that you know will lose money from time to time, is because the power that controls the universe uses bear markets (money losing periods of time) to weed out the weak hands.

"Before you invest, you must ensure that you have realistically assessed your probability of being right and how you will react to the consequences of being wrong."

-Benjamin Graham

Investing Myth #8

⚜

I can just use past returns to decide where I should invest my money

Investing is all about managing uncertainty. You have a goal you are investing for and the problem is no one can predict what future returns will be.

It's mathematically impossible to predict the future price movements of stocks and bonds with absolute certainty.

It's like trying to predict exactly when someone is going to die.

There's no way for life insurance companies to know exactly when a 30-year old male will die.

However, by calculating probabilities and using diversification they can come up with an appropriate premium to charge one thousand 30-year old males.

What does this have to do with investing?

"Monte Carlo simulation" is a process that insurance companies and investment advisory firms use to manage uncertainty.

What is Monte Carlo simulation and how is it used in investing?

Let's assume you wrote down on little sheets of paper each year's return for U.S. large company stocks going back decades.

Then you put those sheets of paper into a bowl and shook them up.

Next you reach in the bowl blindfolded and pull out a return. That return would be your assumption for year one of the simulation you are running.

Each time you take a sheet out, you record the returns in your simulation software in the order you take them out of the bowl. You keep doing this until you have all the annual return assumptions you need.

For example: if you are projecting out 30 years, you need to pull out 30 sheets with annual returns on them one by one.

After you complete that process for all the years you need, then you repeat this process from the beginning (shaking up the returns in the bowl and pulling them out one by one) 1,000 times to create 1,000 potential random outcomes.

What you will end up with is an outcome that shows how many times out of 1,000 random tests you will reach your desired financial goal.

Now here's how you put it all together to build your target portfolio.

You don't actually do this process for one asset class (U.S. large companies stocks). You run this simulation for your specific portfolio asset mix, or the portfolio mix you want to test.

Here's an example of what I mean by portfolio mix:

- *50% U.S. stocks*
- *30% International developed stocks*
- *10% Emerging market stocks*
- *10% U.S. immediate term bonds*

You would run that portfolio through the simulation to see how many times out of 1,000 random scenarios that portfolio allows you to reach your financial goals.

The higher number, the higher the probability you will reach your goal, according to the simulation.

"The contracts (complex annuities) are huge, obtuse, confusing and hence rarely read. Sales reps rarely realize the lies they peddle, singing false praises--because they're paid hugely for a blind eye--that hide obscenely gargantuan commissions."

-Ken Fisher

Investing Myth #9

⚜

I can get stock market returns without stock market risk

When most investors hear this (normally from an annuity salesperson), they initially think, "This sounds too good to be true."

That's your inner common sense talking because it IS too good to be true.

Before I go a little technical, think about this for a second. If insurance companies actually could earn stock market returns without stock market risk, why would so many very smart investors like Warren Buffett, Ray Dalio, George Soros, Paul Tudor Jones, and many other wealthy investors still invest in the actual stock market? (They know a whole lot more about money and investing than the not so smart, insurance agents who peddle this myth.)

Because... you cannot get stock market returns without stock market risk. Just like you can't get in shape without the pain of exercise and eating right.

There are no shortcuts to any worthwhile goal in life.

I believe you intuitively already know this. I just want to give you some background to help put some facts behind your intuition.

Let's start with understanding where your money goes when you invest in these products.

Your money goes into an insurance company's general account. What's that?

It's where insurers deposit premiums they receive from the policies they put in place. Some of the money goes to pay business expenses. Some of the money is set aside to pay for any claims that may come up in the short term. The remaining money is invested so the insurance company can make a profit while they wait to pay any longer term claims.

Insurance regulators place strict restrictions on how aggressive general account investment portfolios can be. They don't want insurance companies getting too aggressive and not having money when the insurance company needs to back a promise it made to a customer.

I've looked at many insurance company general portfolios (especially the ones selling these type of annuities). The majority of their money is in bonds.

There have been plenty of studies that show over the long term a mostly bond portfolio has not grown more than a mostly stock portfolio (**See Investing Myth #3**).

Then how do insurance companies turn "water into wine?" … They don't.

In my opinion, this is just a sales gimmick some insurance agents use to make money.

To make sure I was knowledgeable when speaking about the product, I took the product apart and figured out how it worked.

Insurance companies create this product using a complex interest rate crediting system based on the movement of a specific stock market index. They aren't actually investing your money in the index.

It's like you betting on an NFL game. You don't have to actually play in the game to participate in the bet. The game is just what is used to determine the results of the bet.

In the financial services world, where there's complexity, there's opportunity for the sellers of complex products to make lots of money. If you don't take anything else away from this lesson, remember this.

The math they use to create this complex interest rate crediting system was designed to not credit more than the mostly bond portfolio earns on average over time. If they did, the company would go out of business (Business 101: Your expenses can't be higher than your revenue for too long.)

You can get an idea of what bonds are likely going to earn by looking at their yield.

For example, the 30 year U.S. government bond yield (insurance companies own lots of government bonds) was paying around 8.26% at the beginning of 1990 (**http://www.multpl.com/30-year-treasury-rate/table**).

Compare that to Dimensional Fund Advisors 2017 Matrix Books data which shows U.S. long-term government bonds actual returns from 1990 to the end of 2016 were about 7.9%. Pretty close to the 30-year bond yield at the beginning of 1990 as expected.

The 30-year U.S. government bond yield is right now (as I write this January 21, 2018) at 2.937%. While insurance companies own more than U.S. government bonds, they are a big portion of their general account investments. The other types of bonds they own are mostly low credit risk and have not historically earned significantly more than the U.S. government bonds.

That means owners of these annuity contracts can reasonably assume these annuities won't do as well as they might have been led to believe.

I'm not saying these are horrible products. In a previous post, you might remember me pointing out an old Jewish manuscript that forms my big picture wealth building philosophy - ⅓ of my money in stocks, ⅓ of my money in real estate, and ⅓ of my money in cash and bonds.

For me, I see these types of contracts fitting in my cash and bonds bucket.

My beef is with the misrepresentation of these products by some insurance agents. That's it.

P.S. This logic also applies to index universal life insurance.

"He that is good for making excuses is seldom good for anything else."

-Benjamin Franklin

Investing Myth #10

⚜

I have plenty of time to get serious about investing

There's always a reason not to save and invest. Every financially successful person I've met is a saver and directly attributes the ability to save and invest wisely to their success.

I've categorized many of the excuses I've heard over the years and organized them by age.

As you will see, at 65 or 70 or when you need money (or may no longer want or be able to hustle to get it), you will either have accumulated or you won't. That's up to you. No one is going to do it for you.

Reasons at 22:

- I have plenty of time.
- I'm just getting started. I'm going to wait until I'm making more money.
- I first need to pay off all of my debt before I save anything.
- I'm not sure what I want yet, so I'm going to wait to save and invest until I have concrete goals.
- I don't know enough to start.

Reasons at 32:

- I'm still not done paying off my student loans and now I have a car loan, I'm getting married, and then we want to buy a home. We will start saving and investing after that.
- I'm thinking about changing careers or starting my own business. I'm going to wait until I decide what my next step is.
- I don't have enough money to even start.
- I don't know enough to start.

Reasons at 42:

- It's next to impossible to save anything with these kids. They need something every week.
- We have to buy a new home to accommodate our bigger family, and then we will get serious about investing.
- I put some money in my 401(k). I should be okay with that and social security based on the 5-minute analysis my 401(k) provider gave me.
- I like enjoying life. I don't want to die and have all this money saved up and didn't experience life. (The rationalizing begins)
- I don't know enough to start.

Reasons at 52:

- I literally don't have it. My kids are in college now and they clean me out every month. When they are all through college I can buckle down and get on track.
- Isn't it pointless now? There's no way I can retire since I don't have much saved. I'm just going to tuck my head in the ground and ignore the problem. (Denial of the problem: This is not the actual verbiage, but this is what's being communicated non-verbally.)
- I don't know enough to start.

Reasons at 62:

- You know what. I can live on what social security will provide. I can downsize and not do much. I would be happy living this way, even though almost my entire life I've never lived this way (The ultimate rationalization statement. Another exaggeration of the verbiage, but what is communicated.)

Look, everyone has their own challenges, but as I learned from some friends in college, "Excuses are tools of the incompetent used to build monuments of nothingness."

There will always be a reason not to save and invest money. The people I've met who are successfully building wealth for themselves and their families adopted a simple philosophy. They paid themselves first (or second if they tithe) systematically every single month, no matter what.

You don't have to start big. Just start doing something on some basis that's meaningful, but doable.

If you wanted to train for a marathon and you've never run even a 5K before, you don't decide day one to try to run 5 miles. Even if you did, after the first or second run and the new challenge motivation wore off, you would struggle to keep up that routine because you would have started too strong.

The way you train for a marathon is to wake up the first day and just run as much as you feel like running. Nothing too straining. Then you would stop when you didn't feel like running any more. Make that distance your baseline and never run anything less than that distance for a couple of weeks. Then you slowly build up adding more distance periodically until you're on pace to be in marathon shape.

You can follow the same process when starting your saving and investing program.

Don't let the lifestyle know you want to live turn into you rationalizing why you don't need to have that lifestyle. There's very little that we actually ever need, and I don't know anyone who truly wants to live life with only what they need.

No matter your age now or your income, start your program. You won't regret it later.

I've never met anyone who has said, "Man I started investing way too early."

✣

PART 2

HOW TO BUILD AN INVESTMENT PORTFOLIO FOR RETIREMENT

The Portfolio Planning Process

Step 1:

Create a budget and get an idea of how much money you need monthly to live comfortably. Not just to get by. Who wants to sacrifice and save all this money just to get by?

Plus, it's better to have planned and saved too much money than too little. If you saved too little, there's not much you can do about it when you want to (or are forced to) retire.

Step 2:

Subtract from your monthly income need the amount of income you expect to receive from social security, pension plans, or any other income source you feel very strongly you will have coming in.

Don't use pipe dream income sources. For example: You plan to make great real estate investments that will pay you $5,000 per month. If you already own the properties and they will be paid off before retirement, then it's okay to use that income.

Just remember, it's better to be conservative with your numbers because if you are off, it only hurts you.

Step 3:

Add up all the money you've saved so far for retirement.

Step 4:

Run portfolio comparisons through a Monte Carlo simulation to get an idea of the portfolio mix that gives you the highest probability of reaching your goals (according to the simulation.... see Investing Myth #8).

Where do you get portfolio options to review?

The time saving way is to call up 5 to 10 major mutual fund companies and ask them which global portfolio mix of their funds would they recommend to a conservative, moderate and aggressive investor. Don't worry if you want to use their funds or not. You are just trying to get an idea of a professional global asset allocation mix.

Plug each of those fund mixes into the Monte Carlo simulation and get an idea of the probability each portfolio will allow you to pull out the income you want in retirement without running out of money.

Where do you get the software to build a Monte Carlo analysis? I pay a lot of money to license the software so unless you know how to program and have a lot of time, you are going to have to go a financial advisor that has access to the software and pay them to run it for you. There are also some free online versions, but take them with a grain of salt. They aren't as robust.

Step 5:

Stress test your portfolio and plan a little more by running simulations of big risks that could blow a hole in your plan (You will also need to program this or go to a financial advisor.)

Here are a few examples:

- Social Security getting cut
- Your pension income being cut
- Higher inflation than expected
- Lower returns than expected
- Getting hit with big down years now
- Getting hit with big down years right after you retire
- Higher health care expenses than expected
- Die early
- Live a lot longer than life expectancy

At this point you should have an idea of your target or benchmark portfolio (the asset mix that has a high probability of helping you reach your goals). Now it's time to select the actual investments for your portfolio.

The Investment Selection Process

Most people are aware of the 80/20 principle (Google it). The majority of results and rewards come from a small minority of inputs.

This principle also applies to investing, except the gap is wider. There was a paper done in 1986 called "Determinants of Portfolio Performance" by Gary Brinson, L. Randolph Hood and Gilbert Beebower (Financial Analysts Journal, July/August 1986...Feel free to google it and read all the details of the study on your own.)

The paper showed that a portfolio's target asset allocation (what percentage of your money is in stocks, bonds or cash) accounted for about 93% of its return. Stock picking, market timing and all other inputs to portfolio management accounted for the other 7% combined.

This is not to say that no one can time the market or become a superior stock picker. After all, Warren Buffett is one of the best stock pickers of all time.

What it does make clear to me is that there's a lot more effective way to achieve the investment results I need to achieve my long-term financial goals with way less stress.

Plus, if you tell me I can capture the majority of the upside of investing in the stock market, while being able to eliminate single stock risk through diversification (My definition: own thousands of stocks around the world), then sign me up.

When you put your money in any asset class it's never fully safe. I have not yet had anyone give me a situation where if all the stocks in my globally diversified portfolio go to zero, then cash in the bank would be safe.

I'm not saying it's not possible. I guess anything is possible. It's just not very probable (and again I have yet to find anyone to give me one idea that would at least make it possible).

If the economic system ever does break down, then your money isn't safe anywhere. So, you don't need to worry about that.

Focus on positioning yourself to weather short-term economic down-turns that could affect single companies, industries or countries, by building a well-diversified global portfolio of stocks (and bonds if you need to dampen the up and down movements and you don't mind making less money over time).

The way I like to diversify is by building my portfolio using exchange traded funds, ETFs. ETFs are just a basket of securities organized into categories. For example, you have

ETFs for U.S. stocks, ETFs for value stocks, ETFs for emerging market stocks, and even ETFs for marijuana stocks!

Just about any stock or bond category has an ETF that allows you to get that asset class into your portfolio without you having to take a single security risk.

Now let's go back to the work you did in the portfolio planning process. Let's assume your target portfolio asset mix ended up looking something like this:

- Large Cap Value: 15%
- Large Cap Growth: 15%
- Mid Cap: 10%
- Small Cap: 5%
- International Developed: 25%
- International Emerging: 10%
- Intermediate Term Bonds: 20%

All you have to do now is go find ETFs that can fit within each asset class. This is going to require you doing your research. You don't want to just look at the name of the fund.

You want to read the prospectus and see what it's actually investing in to be sure it fits your asset class category.

I can write an entire book on the different types of ETFs and how to select them. It seems like there are new ETFs coming out every week.

Don't become discouraged if you get overwhelmed. Take your time. Do your research. If you don't have the time, then I really recommend you find a financial advisor to help you through the process.

Ongoing Portfolio Management

Most people have heard of the buy and hold investment strategy. I personally don't believe that this is the best strategy.

At the very least you want to buy and rebalance. That means, pick a time (once a year, once a quarter, etc.) to review your portfolio and adjust all the asset classes back to the target portfolio.

As markets move, your portfolio percentages will get out of whack. This keeps the portfolio on track with your planned asset mix.

I like to take it a step further when managing my money and my client's money.

I will make an adjustment to the portfolio if my client's plan, which we are reviewing and running through a Monte Carlo simulation, at least annually, changes.

Something may happen to their financial situation that may increase or decrease the probability of their current portfolio helping them reach their goals.

Markets also trend. If you can understand the trend and put more of your money in the types of assets that do best in that trend, you have a high probability of making more money than your target portfolio over that trending period.

If you want to understand market trends and how to profit from them, you must do your homework. I'm constantly researching cause and effect relationships in the markets to create rules for my investment process, that allow me to take emotion out of the investing and make decisions based on odds and probabilities. A systematic approach to investing versus relying on "gut feel".

Some years my system will be right and beat the benchmark portfolio. Some years my system will be wrong, and it will get beat.

If we're making decisions based on the odds being in our favor, then net over time, we should outperform.

However, nothing is guaranteed. So, we don't like to deviate that far from the target portfolio, unless we see something that everyone else is really ignoring (which is extremely hard to do).

❧

Part 3

Why Most Investors Underperform Their Own Investments

"The most important quality for an investor is temperament, not intellect. You need a temperament that neither derives great pleasure from being with the crowd or against the crowd."

-Warren Buffett

When I first started in the investment business 10 years ago, I was introduced to a study that showed how the average investor under-performed their own investments by a significant margin.

The study was given to me by a mutual fund company. Since then, I've seen and heard about the same studies being done by hedge funds, private equity funds, individuals, and many other investment vehicles with the same outcomes (the investor under-performing their own investments).

I remember reading the first study, thinking, "Wait, how do the investors in these funds earn less money than the funds earned over this time period?"

I knew the fees of the fund, and the difference wasn't all fees. Over time, I learned it was mistakes in the investor's behavior that caused them to earn less than the investments they were investing in over time.

Why is this important?

Just about everyone I talk to thinks there is a lack of good investment options available. Many feel they have to be part of the "in" crowd to find a good investment opportunity.

Nothing could be further from the truth. Just do your own research and pick a major mutual fund company you know. Look at the 10 and 20 year returns of their U.S. large cap fund (this type of fund is comprised of big established companies in the U.S., nothing fancy) returns and you will see the returns are better than what most investors earn over time.

It's my belief that if investors can identify the common investor mistakes made, and set up systems and processes to help them minimize or eliminate their mistakes, they will end up closing the gap between what their investment earns and what the actual investor earns.

There are many behavioral mistakes that I've observed and read about over the years. I'm going to just take four of the most common ones I run into all the time as examples.

Lack of Proper Diversification

I read about an investment advisor who had a client who wanted to fire him in 1999 because his diversified portfolio was only up 25% and his friend who had a different portfolio concentrated in tech stocks was up over 100%.

If that client followed through on firing his advisor and chased his friend's portfolio, we know how that ended (Go look at a chart of the NASDAQ from 1999 to 2002.)

Here's one of the best ways I've heard diversification described, "Diversification isn't going to make you a killing, but it will make sure you don't get killed."

Overconfidence

You can call this pride as well. This mistake starts to rear its ugly head late into a bull market. Investors begin to look at how far the market has risen, their fears of losing money begin to go away and they read books that give the impression that investing successfully and making millions is easy.

Amateur investors begin to believe they can time the market or select superior investments with only 30 minutes of research done per week (if that). The penny stock seminars start filling up, amateur home flippers begin to crowd the marketplace, and many people who haven't had the proper investment training become day traders.

Many of these investors may even make money for a time and brag to their friends at dinner parties or at the gym until... that inevitable time when the market humbles them, and they give back all the money they made and more.

Fear

I meet someone almost every week who tells me about how much money they lost in 2008 and how that caused them to sit out the markets for a few years.

That's unfortunate because I show them the price of the S&P 500 (my proxy for the overall stock market) at the low February 2009 at 734.52 and how the S&P 500 has basically tripled since then (the day of this writing January 24, 2018 the S&P is at 2842).

What that means is if they had a broadly diversified portfolio and didn't give in to their fears and thoughts that "this time it's different," they would have made a lot of money over the last few years.

This time has yet to be different, but in times of uncertainty, fear can grab hold of us and cause us to make some bad decisions.

Gambling and Calling it Investing

One of my closest friends told me he bought Tesla stock and asked my opinion of the stock after the fact. I asked him what made him buy the stock. His answer was the car was so awesome the stock had to go up.

I asked him a series of questions about the process he used to make his investments and the basic conclusion was that he didn't have one.

"My definition of gambling is when you make investment decisions without knowing the odds of making money or losing money."

The only way to know the odds is to have a plan and a process that helps you determine that.

When people gamble at casinos, the odds are not in their favor to make money. They may get lucky, but the more they play, the more money the casino takes out of their pocket.

That's why casinos and state lotteries are such profitable schemes (yes, I intentionally chose the word scheme.) There's a gambler in all of us and many investors I meet let that gambler out when they are investing and don't even realize the gambler is running the show. The gambler inside of us is probably the most dangerous of the mistake creators because the gambler causes many investors to lose everything when he/she is able to take full control over the investing process.

We are all human and are exposed to human error. As a matter of fact, it's very easy to see the mistakes other investors are making, but it is pretty hard to notice when you are in the process of making one of the mistakes yourself, until after the damage is done.

No one is immune (not even money managers like myself). That's why I'm a big fan of accountability. I mean if Warren Buffett has Charlie Munger to help him minimize the mistakes he makes, (and he's one of the best investors of all time) why shouldn't I have someone to help me.

An accountability partner can be a friend, family member, (someone not in the same household) or a wealth manager/financial adviser. Just make sure they are knowledgeable about investing and have a similar investment philosophy as the one you follow.

Conclusion

That's it. I have nothing else for you. You have what you need to build a successful investing plan for retirement.

"Feel free to look me up by name on Facebook and LinkedIn and on Instagram @askphillip. I put out lots of free information on business, investing, and financial planning.

Thanks for buying my book and reading it all the way through. If it brought you value share please it with a friend or buy them their own copy.

I wish you success in investing for your future."

About the Author

Before starting his own firm, Phillip Washington earned a finance degree from the University of Texas at San Antonio, and worked as a financial adviser for a large financial services company for 8 years. He also spent two years on an investment committee at a boutique registered investment advisory firm where they managed a little over $90 million.

He later started his own firm, Stone Hill Wealth Management, and today his clients hire his firm to help them make many important financial decisions (i.e., investing, money management, estate planning, exit planning for a business or joint venture, buying a home, car, rental property, etc.).

Phillip lives in Grand Prairie, Texas with his amazing wife, Kelley, and his two smart and energetic boys, Tate and Kellen.

www.ingramcontent.com/pod-product-compliance
Lightning Source LLC
Chambersburg PA
CBHW061049220326
41597CB00018BA/2722